Pretzel Cookbook

The Perfect Collection of Crunchy Salty and Sweet Pretzel Recipes

BY - Charlotte Long

© 2022 Charlotte Long. All rights reserved.

License Page

No part of this book and its content should be transmitted in any format for commercial and personal use without asking for permission from the author in writing.

The purpose of the content is to enlighten you and pass cooking knowledge to you in a straightforward way. Hence, the author is not responsible for any implications and assumptions drawn from the book and its content.

♡♡♡♡♡♡♡♡♡♡♡♡♡♡♡

Table of Contents

Introduction 6

Pretzel Recipes 8

   1. Choco Dipped Pretzels 9

   2. Cinnamon Sugar Pretzels 12

   3. Philly Cheesesteak Pretzels 15

   4. Cheeseburger Pretzels 18

   5. Crunchy Pretzel Rods 22

   6. Chocolate-Dipped Hard Pretzels 25

   7. White Chocolate Covered Pretzels with Sprinkles 28

   8. Cheese Dipped Pretzels 31

   9. Breakfast Pretzels 34

   10. Biscoff Spread Pretzel Bites 37

   11. Custard Pretzel Bites 40

   12. Jelly Pretzel Bites 44

   13. Baklava Pretzel Bites 47

   14. Mascarpone and Fig Pretzel Bites 50

   15. Crunchy Cheesy Pretzel Bites 53

   16. Sparkling White Chocolate Pretzels 56

   17. Strawberry Layered Pretzel Dessert 58

   18. Strawberry Pretzel Party Popsicles 61

19. Swedish Sugared Sweet Pretzels 63

20. White Chocolate and Pink Peppercorn Pretzels 67

21. White Chocolate Haystacks 69

22. Yogurt Glazed Pretzels 71

23. Vegan Heart... 73

24. The Herbal Knot 76

25. The Perfect Appetizer 79

26. The Big Delight 82

27. Mini Coco Bites 85

28. The Classic Cheese Pretzels 87

29. Pretzel Pie... 90

30. Pretzel Cake... 92

31. Pretzel Eggs.. 94

32. Pretzel Bratwurst Bites 96

33. Homemade Pretzels 99

34. Pretzel Salad... 102

35. Pretzel Bread 105

36. Sugar Pretzels 108

37. Pretzel Buns.. 111

38. Gluten-Free Pretzels 114

39. DSF's Pretzel Bread 117

40. Betty's Pretzels 120

41. Bacon-Wrapped Pretzels 122

42. Chocolate Pretzels 124

43. Pretzels with Coconut and Cream Cheese 126

44. Caramel Pretzel Bites 129

45. Cheesy Garlic Pull Apart Pretzels 132

46. Parmesan Crusted Soft Pretzels 135

47. Pizza Pretzel Bites 138

48. Pretzel Toffee 141

49. Peppermint Pretzel Dippers 143

50. Pineapple Pretzel Fluff 145

51. Coco Pretzels 147

Conclusion 150

Epilogues 151

Introduction

Pretzel lovers, rejoice! If you're looking for something to satisfy your cravings for the perfect puffy, crunchy, chewy sweet and salty snack, then look no further than this cookbook.

The cookbook is a collection of delicious recipes for anyone who loves pretzels. We've compiled our favorite pretzel recipes into an easy to use e-book so that you can enjoy the flavors anytime and anywhere that suit you best.

There are over 50 pretzel recipes inside the cookbook, and we've taken the time to create each one to cater to a wide range of palettes. From savory to sweet twists and more, there's something in here that you will be pleased with.

If you're not sure about anything, the cookbook benefits from having an in-depth explanation to help you get started. So don't worry if you're not too sure about pretzels or even if you have never made them before. We've got an easy to follow guide that will take you through how to make each recipe step by step.

There is a wealth of information inside the cookbook that we can't wait for you to find out about. With so many cool ideas, you'll definitely want to get started on trying them out as soon as possible.

You're going to love all the recipes, which will be great for satisfying your pretzel cravings. Each one has been created with a unique twist and lots of love, so you can feel good about giving it a try.

The variety of recipes inside the cookbook is incredible. It's great to see that we've created so many different pretzels and that you can particularly choose ones that are perfect for you. With some easy-to-follow instructions, it's not long before you are rolling out your dough and getting to work!

There is nothing worse than wasting time and effort when you know that it could've been better spent. With the cookbook, you have nothing to worry about; if anything, you'll be pleased with all the effort that has gone into creating every recipe.

With the recipes, you'll be able to impress your family and friends no end. You'll love how easy they are to make and how quickly they can actually be prepared for a tasty treat. Try some of our recommendations for savory flavor or go for something sweet....

Pretzel Recipes

These recipes are the ideal way to get creative in the kitchen and make something special for everyone to enjoy. You'll be able to create a range of different pretzel shapes and tastes that will be great for everyone. Try some of your own ideas out or stick with some of our recommendations.

1. Choco Dipped Pretzels

Pretzels and gooey molten chocolate? Delicious!

Servings: 8

Preparation Time: 2 Hours 20 Minutes

Ingredients:

- 1 (7g) package active dry yeast
- 1 c. warm water
- 1 tbsp. brown sugar
- 3 ¼ c. bread flour
- ½ c. cold beer
- 2 tbsp. unsalted butter at room temperature, cut into 1" pieces and extra for greasing
- 2 tsp. salt
- 1 c. chocolate chips
- 1 tbsp. butter
- 1 egg yolk + 1 tbsp. water - egg wash

Instructions:

Preheat your oven to 500°F.

In a stand mixer, add the warm water and active dry yeast.

Add in the brown sugar. Mix thoroughly and allow to bloom until foamy. It should take about 5 minutes.

Add the bread flour, unsalted butter, salt and cold beer. Then, stir. At low speed, begin kneading the dough for 1 minute or until it forms a smooth ball. Continue kneading until the dough becomes pliant about 5 minutes.

In a greased bowl, place the dough and cover it with saran wrap. Set away to rise in a warm area for 90 minutes until double in size.

Divide the dough into 8 portions. Then, roll the portions out into a desired shape – knots, buns or sticks.

Arrange on 2 lined baking trays about 2" apart.

Allow rising for 30 more minutes.

Coat with the quick egg wash before baking for 8-10 minutes until crispy and golden brown!

In a saucepan, melt together the chocolate chips and butter until smooth.

To serve, begin dipping the pretzels into the chocolate and lay them on a wax paper-lined tray.

Cool for 20 minutes before serving!

2. Cinnamon Sugar Pretzels

These pretzels are a favorite! The rich cinnamon flavor perfectly balances the crunchy sweetness of sugar.

Servings: 8

Preparation Time: 2 Hour 20 Minutes

Ingredients:

- 1 (7g) package active dry yeast
- 1 c. warm water
- 1 tbsp. brown sugar
- 3 ¼ c. bread flour
- ½ c. cold beer
- 2 tbsp. unsalted butter, cut into 1" pieces plus extra for greasing
- 2 tsp. salt
- ½ c. sugar
- ½ tbsp. cinnamon
- 1 tbsp. butter, melted
- 1 egg yolk + 1 tbsp. water - egg wash

Instructions:

Preheat your oven to 500°F.

In a stand mixer, add the warm water and active dry yeast.

Add in the brown sugar. Mix thoroughly and allow to bloom until foamy. It should take about 5 minutes.

Add the bread flour, unsalted butter, salt and cold beer. Then, stir. At low speed, begin kneading the dough for 1 minute or until it forms a smooth ball. Continue kneading until the dough becomes pliant about 5 minutes.

In a greased bowl, place the dough and cover it with saran wrap. Set away to rise in a warm area for 90 minutes until double in size.

Divide the dough into 8 portions. Then, roll the portions out into a desired shape – knots, buns or sticks.

Arrange on 2 lined baking trays about 2" apart.

Allow rising for 30 more minutes.

Coat with the quick egg wash before baking for 8-10 minutes until crispy and golden brown!

In a bowl, add the sugar and cinnamon, then mix well.

Once the pretzels are baked, remove them from the oven and lightly coat them with the butter while still piping hot. Sprinkle on the cinnamon sugar!

Serve warm!

3. Philly Cheesesteak Pretzels

Everyone's favorite sandwich in a pretzel roll? Count us in!

Servings: 8

Preparation Time: 2 Hours 20 Minutes

Ingredients:

- 1 (7g) package active dry yeast
- 1 c. warm water
- 1 tbsp. brown sugar
- 3 ¼ c. bread flour
- ½ c. cold beer
- 2 tbsp. unsalted butter, cut into 1" pieces plus extra for greasing
- 2 tsp. salt
- 1 egg yolk + 1 tbsp. water - egg wash

Filling:

- 2 tbsp. olive oil
- 1 green bell pepper, thinly sliced
- 1 onion, thinly sliced
- ½ tsp. sea salt
- All-purpose flour for dusting
- 8 oz. roast beef, thinly sliced
- 8 provolone cheese slices

Instructions:

Preheat your oven to 500°F.

To make the filling, heat a large pan with the olive oil. When hot, add in the green bell pepper, onion and sea salt. Cook until brown and tender for about 15 minutes.

Remove from the pan and set aside.

In a stand mixer, add the warm water and active dry yeast.

Add in the brown sugar. Mix thoroughly and allow to bloom until foamy. It should take about 5 minutes.

Add the bread flour, unsalted butter, salt and cold beer. Then, stir. At low speed, begin kneading the dough for 1 minute or until it forms a smooth ball. Continue kneading until the dough becomes pliant about 5 minutes.

In a greased bowl, place the dough and cover it with saran wrap. Set away to rise in a warm area for 90 minutes until double in size.

Divide into 8 equal portions and roll each portion into a large rectangle—approximately 6.5 by 7.5".

With the shorter end at the bottom, layer on one roast beef slice, 2 tablespoons of the filling, and one provolone cheese slice along the lower half. Make sure to leave ½" of the dough border around the filling.

Fold the top of the dough over and press together the edges. Repeat with the remaining dough pieces.

Arrange on 2 lined baking trays about 2" apart.

Allow rising for 30 more minutes.

Coat with the quick egg wash before baking for 8-10 minutes until crispy and golden brown!

Serve warm!

4. Cheeseburger Pretzels

These classic pretzels are great as a starter for any dinner party!

Servings: 8

Preparation Time: 2 Hours 20 Minutes

Ingredients:

- 1 (7g) package active dry yeast
- 1 c. warm water
- 1 tbsp. brown sugar
- 3 ¼ c. bread flour
- 2 tbsp. unsalted butter, cut into 1" pieces, plus extra for greasing
- 2 tsp. salt
- 1 egg yolk + 1 tbsp. water - egg wash

Filling:

- 2 tbsp. olive oil
- 1 green bell pepper, thinly sliced
- 1 onion, thinly sliced
- ½ tsp. sea salt
- 8 oz. cooked beef, minced
- 8 American cheese slices
- Pickles, chopped
- Ketchup
- Mustard

Instructions:

Preheat your oven to 500°F.

To make the filling, heat a large pan with the olive oil. When hot, add in the green bell pepper, onion and sea salt. Cook until brown and tender for about 15 minutes.

Remove from the pan and set aside.

In a stand mixer, add the warm water and active dry yeast.

Add in the brown sugar. Mix thoroughly and allow to bloom until foamy. It should take about 5 minutes.

Add in the bread flour, unsalted butter and salt, then continue stirring. At low speed, begin kneading the dough for 1 minute or until it forms a smooth ball. Continue kneading until the dough become pliant about 5 minutes.

In a greased bowl, place the dough and cover it with saran wrap. Set away to rise in a warm area for 90 minutes until double in size.

Divide the dough into 8 equal portions and roll each portion out into a large rectangle—approximately 6.5 by 7.5".

With the shorter end at the bottom, layer on 1 ounce of the cooked beef, 1 tablespoon of the filling and one American cheese slice. Make sure to leave ½" of the dough border around the filling.

Top with pickles, ketchup and mustard. Then, fold the top over and press together the edges. Repeat the process with the remaining dough rectangles.

Arrange on 2 lined baking trays about 2" apart.

Allow rising for 30 more minutes.

Coat with the quick egg wash before baking for 8-10 minutes until crispy and golden brown!

Serve warm!

5. Crunchy Pretzel Rods

Make these pretzel rods in advance to have a delicious pretzel snack throughout the week.

Servings: 12

Preparation Time: 1 Hour

Ingredients:

- 1 (7g) package active dry yeast
- 1 c. warm water
- 1 tbsp. brown sugar
- 3 ¼ c. all-purpose flour
- 2 tbsp. unsalted butter, cut into 1" pieces, plus extra for greasing
- 2 tsp. salt, plus extra for sprinkling

Instructions:

In a stand mixer, add the warm water and active dry yeast.

Add in the brown sugar. Mix thoroughly and allow to bloom until foamy. It should take about 5 minutes.

Add the all-purpose flour, unsalted butter and salt. Then, stir. At low speed, begin kneading the dough for 1 minute or until it forms a smooth ball. Continue kneading until the dough become pliant about 5 minutes.

In a greased bowl, place the dough and cover it with saran wrap. Then, place in the refrigerator and allow cold rise for 8 hours.

Preheat your oven to 325°F.

Divide the dough into 48 equal portions, then begin rolling each portion out into a long thin shape.

Arrange on 2 lined baking trays about 2" apart.

Allow rising for 30 more minutes.

Sprinkle with salt before baking for 20-30 minutes, testing hardness.

6. Chocolate-Dipped Hard Pretzels

This is a delicious hard pretzel variation with CHOCOLATE! Yum!

Servings: 24

Preparation Time: 1 Hour

Ingredients:

- 1 (7g) package active dry yeast
- 1 c. warm water
- 1 tbsp. brown sugar
- 3 ¼ c. all-purpose flour
- 2 tbsp. unsalted butter, cut into 1" pieces, plus extra for greasing
- 2 tsp. salt, plus extra for sprinkling
- 1 c. dark chocolate chips
- 1 tbsp. butter
- Nuts and sprinkles as needed

Instructions:

In a stand mixer, add the warm water and active dry yeast.

Add in the brown sugar. Mix thoroughly and allow to bloom until foamy. It should take about 5 minutes.

Add in the all-purpose flour, unsalted butter and salt, then continue stirring. At low speed, begin kneading the dough for 1 minute or until it forms a smooth ball. Continue kneading until the dough becomes pliant about 5 minutes.

In a greased bowl, place the dough. Then, cover it with saran wrap. Place in the refrigerator and allow cold rise for 8 hours.

Preheat your oven to 325°F.

Divide the dough into 48 equal portions and begin rolling each portion out into a long thin shape.

Arrange on 2 lined baking trays about 2" apart.

Allow rising for 30 more minutes.

Sprinkle with salt before baking for 20-30 minutes, testing hardness.

In a saucepan, melt together the dark chocolate chips and butter until smooth.

To serve, begin dipping the pretzels into the chocolate and lay them on a wax paper-lined tray. You could now top with nuts or sprinkles if desired.

Cool for 20 minutes before serving!

7. White Chocolate Covered Pretzels with Sprinkles

Kids are going to love these pretzels! They call for white chocolate and sprinkles!

Servings: 8

Preparation Time: 2 Hours 20 Minutes

Ingredients:

- 1 (7g) package active dry yeast
- 1 c. warm water
- 1 tbsp. brown sugar
- 3 ¼ c. bread flour
- ½ c. cold beer
- 2 tbsp. unsalted butter, cut into 1" pieces plus extra for greasing
- 2 tsp. salt
- 1 c. white chocolate chips
- 1 tbsp. butter
- ½ c. sprinkles
- 1 egg yolk + 1 tbsp. water - egg wash

Instructions:

Preheat your oven to 500°F.

In a stand mixer, add the warm water and active dry yeast.

Add in the brown sugar. Mix thoroughly and allow to bloom until foamy. It should take about 5 minutes.

Add the bread flour, unsalted butter, salt and cold beer. Then, stir. At low speed, begin kneading the dough for a minute or until it forms a smooth ball. Continue kneading until the dough become pliant about 5 minutes.

In a greased bowl, place the dough and cover it with saran wrap. Set away to rise in a warm area for 90 minutes until double in size.

Divide the dough into 8 portions. Then, roll the portions out into a desired shape – knots, buns or sticks.

Arrange on 2 lined baking trays about 2" apart.

Allow rising for 30 more minutes.

Coat with the quick egg wash before baking for 8-10 minutes until crispy and golden brown!

In a saucepan, melt together the white chocolate chips and butter until smooth.

To serve, begin dipping the pretzels into the chocolate and lay them on a wax paper-lined tray. Toss on the sprinkles while still wet.

Set for 20 minutes before serving!

8. Cheese Dipped Pretzels

These pretzels are absolutely delicious for any game night!

Servings: 8

Preparation Time: 2 Hours 20 Minutes

Ingredients:

- 1 (7g) package active dry yeast
- 1 c. warm water
- 1 tbsp. brown sugar
- 3 ¼ c. bread flour
- ½ c. cold beer
- 2 tbsp. unsalted butter, cut into 1" pieces plus extra for greasing
- 2 tsp. salt
- 1 c. cheddar cheese, grated and melted
- 1 egg yolk + 1 tbsp. water - egg wash

Instructions:

Preheat your oven to 500°F.

In a stand mixer, add the warm water and active dry yeast.

Add in the brown sugar. Mix thoroughly and allow to bloom until foamy. It should take about 5 minutes.

Add the bread flour, unsalted butter, salt and cold beer. Then, stir. At low speed, begin kneading the dough for a minute or until it forms a smooth ball. Continue kneading until the dough become pliant about 5 minutes.

In a greased bowl, place the dough and cover it with saran wrap. Set away to rise in a warm area for 90 minutes until double in size.

Divide the dough into 8 portions. Then, roll the portions out into a desired shape – knots, buns or sticks.

Arrange on 2 lined baking trays about 2" apart.

Allow rising for 30 more minutes.

Coat with the quick egg wash before baking for 8-10 minutes until crispy and golden brown!

To serve, begin dipping the pretzels into the cheddar cheese and lay them on a wax paper-lined tray.

Set for 20 minutes before serving!

9. Breakfast Pretzels

You can make these pretzels the night before and simply pop them into the oven for 5 minutes for a delicious and quick breakfast!

Servings: 8

Preparation Time: 2 Hours 10 Minutes

Ingredients:

- 1 (7g) package active dry yeast
- 1 c. warm water
- 1 tbsp. brown sugar
- 2 c. bread flour
- 1 ¼ c. spelt flour
- 1/3 c. cold beer
- 2 tbsp. unsalted butter, cut into 1" pieces
- 2 tsp. salt
- 1 large tomato, chopped
- ½ c. cheddar cheese, grated
- 1 tbsp. fresh basil
- 1 egg yolk + 1 tbsp. water - egg wash

Instructions:

Preheat your oven to 500°F.

In a stand mixer, add the warm water and active dry yeast.

Add in the brown sugar. Mix thoroughly and allow to bloom until foamy. It should take about 5 minutes.

Add the flours, unsalted butter, salt and cold beer. Then, stir. At low speed, begin kneading the dough for a minute or until it forms a smooth ball.

Add in the large tomato, cheddar cheese and fresh basil, then continue kneading until the dough become pliant about 5 minutes.

In a greased bowl, place the dough and cover it with saran wrap. Set away to rise in a warm area for 90 minutes until double in size.

Divide the dough into 8 portions. Then, roll the portions out into a desired shape – knots, buns or sticks.

Arrange on 2 lined baking trays about 2" apart.

Allow rising for 30 more minutes.

Coat with the quick egg wash before baking for 8-10 minutes until crispy and golden brown!

Serve warm!

10. Biscoff Spread Pretzel Bites

Melty cookie spread inside a pretzel bun! You heard that right!

Servings: 12

Preparation Time: 2 Hours 20 Minutes

Ingredients:

- 1 (7g) package active dry yeast
- 1 c. warm water
- 1 tbsp. brown sugar
- 3 ¼ c. bread flour
- ½ c. cold milk
- 2 tbsp. unsalted butter, cut into 1" pieces, plus extra for greasing
- 2 tsp. salt
- 1 ½ c. Biscoff spread
- 1 egg yolk + 1 tbsp. water - egg wash

Instructions:

Preheat your oven to 500°F.

In a stand mixer, add the warm water and active dry yeast.

Add in the brown sugar. Mix thoroughly and allow to bloom until foamy. It should take about 5 minutes.

Add in the bread flour, unsalted butter, cold milk and salt, then continue stirring. At low speed, begin kneading the dough for 1 minute or until it forms a smooth ball. Continue kneading until the dough become pliant about 5 minutes.

In a greased bowl, place the dough and cover it with saran wrap. Set away to rise in a warm area for 90 minutes until double in size.

Place the dough on a floured counter and divide it into 12 equal portions.

Roll each portion into a rectangle. Then, place about 2 tablespoons of the Biscoff spread in the center.

Pull the edges together and pinch them to cover. Ensure the filling is completely covered and set onto a baking tray.

Repeat the process with the remaining dough rectangles. Place them 2" apart.

Allow rising for 30 more minutes.

Coat with the quick egg wash before baking for 8-10 minutes until crispy and golden brown!

11. Custard Pretzel Bites

The delicious homemade custard makes for a beautiful filling for these pretzel bites!

Servings: 12

Preparation Time: 2 Hours 20 Minutes

Ingredients:

- 1 (7g) package active dry yeast
- 1 c. warm water
- 1 tbsp. brown sugar
- 3 ¼ c. bread flour
- ½ c. cold milk
- 2 tbsp. unsalted butter, cut into 1" pieces plus extra for greasing
- 2 tsp. salt
- 1 egg yolk + 1 tbsp. water - egg wash

Filling:

- 2/3 c. cornstarch
- 2/3 c. custard powder
- 2/3 c. sugar
- 3 1/3 c. milk
- 1 tbsp. vanilla extract
- 1 ½ c. thick cream
- ¼ c. butter
- 3 egg yolks
- 2/3 c. pistachios, chopped

Instructions:

Preheat your oven to 500°F.

In a stand mixer, add the warm water and active dry yeast.

Add in the brown sugar. Mix thoroughly and allow to bloom until foamy. It should take about 5 minutes.

Add in the bread flour, unsalted butter, cold milk and salt, then continue stirring. At low speed, begin kneading the dough for 1 minute or until it forms a smooth ball. Continue kneading until the dough become pliant about 5 minutes.

In a greased bowl, place the dough and cover it with saran wrap. Set away to rise in a warm area for 90 minutes until double in size.

To make the filling, combine the cornstarch, custard powder and sugar in a saucepan, then mix well. Add the milk, vanilla extract and thick cream. Stir the mixture over low heat until it has cooked and thickened. Add the butter. Cook for 5 minutes, continue stirring the mixture.

Remove the saucepan from the heat. Stir in the egg yolks.

Add the pistachios, then combine. Cover the custard and leave it to cool completely.

Once the dough rises, place it on a floured counter and divide it into 12 equal portions.

Roll each portion into a rectangle. Then, place about 2 tablespoons of the filling in the center.

Pull the edges together and pinch them to cover. Ensure the filling is completely covered and set onto a baking tray.

Repeat the process with the remaining dough rectangles. Place them 2" apart.

Allow rising for 30 more minutes.

Coat with the quick egg wash before baking for 8-10 minutes until crispy and golden brown!

12. Jelly Pretzel Bites

Make your jelly or use a store brought one if you're in a hurry! This recipe works well either way!

Servings: 24

Preparation Time: 2 Hours 30 Minutes

Ingredients:

- 1 (7g) package active dry yeast
- 1 c. warm water
- 1 tbsp. brown sugar
- 3 ¼ c. bread flour
- ½ c. cold milk
- 2 tbsp. unsalted butter, cut into 1 "pieces plus extra for greasing
- 2 tsp. salt
- 1 egg yolk + 1 tbsp. water - egg wash

Filling:

- 1 c. strawberries, chopped
- ½ c. sugar
- 1 gelatin sheet, bloomed

Instructions:

Preheat your oven to 500°F.

In a stand mixer, add the warm water and active dry yeast.

Add in the brown sugar. Mix thoroughly and allow to bloom until foamy. It should take about 5 minutes.

Add in the bread flour, unsalted butter, cold milk and salt, then continue stirring. At low speed, begin kneading the dough for 1 minute or until it forms a smooth ball. Continue kneading until the dough become pliant about 5 minutes.

In a greased bowl, place the dough and cover it with saran wrap. Set away to rise in a warm area for 90 minutes until double in size.

To make the filling, combine all the ingredients in a saucepan and cook until the strawberries crush. Cool completely.

Once the dough rises, place it on a floured counter and divide it into 12 equal portions. Then, divide each portion into 2 pieces for 24 pieces.

Roll each piece into a rectangle. Then, place about 1 tablespoon of the filling in the center.

Pull the edges together and pinch them to cover. Ensure the filling is completely covered and set onto a baking tray.

Repeat the process with the remaining dough rectangles. Place them 2" apart.

Allow rising for 30 more minutes.

Coat with the quick egg wash before baking for 8-10 minutes until crispy and golden brown!

13. Baklava Pretzel Bites

The delicious Middle Eastern inspired filling takes these pretzel bites to another level!

Servings: 24

Preparation Time: 2 Hours 20 Minutes

Ingredients:

- 1 (7g) package active dry yeast
- 1 c. warm water
- 1 tbsp. brown sugar
- 3 ¼ c. bread flour
- ½ c. cold milk
- 2 tbsp. unsalted butter, cut into 1" pieces plus extra for greasing
- 2 tsp. salt
- ½ c. walnuts, chopped
- ½ c. pistachios, chopped
- ½ c. honey
- 1 egg yolk + 1 tbsp. water - egg wash

Instructions:

Preheat your oven to 500°F.

In a stand mixer, add the warm water and active dry yeast.

Add in the brown sugar. Mix thoroughly and allow to bloom until foamy. It should take about 5 minutes.

Add in the bread flour, unsalted butter, cold milk and salt, then continue stirring. At low speed, begin kneading the dough for 1 minute or until it forms a smooth ball. Continue kneading until the dough become pliant about 5 minutes.

In a greased bowl, place the dough and cover it with saran wrap. Set away to rise in a warm area for 90 minutes until double in size.

To make the filling, combine the nuts and honey. Set aside.

Once the dough rises, place it on a floured counter and divide it into 12 equal portions. Then, divide each portion into 2 pieces for 24 pieces.

Roll each piece into a rectangle. Then, place about 1 tablespoon of the filling in the center.

Pull the edges together and pinch them to cover. Ensure the filling is completely covered and set onto a baking tray.

Repeat the process with the remaining dough rectangles. Place them 2" apart.

Allow rising for 30 more minutes.

Coat with the quick egg wash before baking for 8-10 minutes until crispy and golden brown!

14. Mascarpone and Fig Pretzel Bites

Looking for a unique appetizer? Try out these delicious pretzel bites!

Servings: 12

Preparation Time: 2 Hours 40 Minutes

Ingredients:

- 1 (7g) package active dry yeast
- 1 c. warm water
- 1 tbsp. brown sugar
- 3 ¼ c. bread flour
- ½ c. cold milk
- 2 tbsp. unsalted butter, cut into 1" pieces plus extra for greasing
- 2 tsp. salt
- 1 ½ c. mascarpone cheese, whipped
- ½ c. fig slices
- 1 egg yolk + 1 tbsp. water - egg wash

Instructions:

Preheat your oven to 500°F.

In a stand mixer, add the warm water and active dry yeast.

Add in the brown sugar. Mix thoroughly and allow to bloom until foamy. It should take about 5 minutes.

Add in the bread flour, unsalted butter, cold milk and salt, then continue stirring. At low speed, begin kneading the dough for 1 minute or until it forms a smooth ball. Continue kneading until the dough become pliant about 5 minutes.

In a greased bowl, place the dough and cover it with saran wrap. Set away to rise in a warm area for 90 minutes until double in size. Divide the dough into 12 pieces.

Roll each piece into a rectangle. Place about 2 tablespoons of the mascarpone cheese in the center and top with one fig slice.

Pull the edges together and pinch to cover. Ensure the filling is completely covered and set onto a baking tray.

Repeat the process with the remaining dough rectangles. Place them 2" apart.

Allow rising for 30 more minutes.

Coat with the quick egg wash before baking for 10 minutes until crispy and golden brown!

15. Crunchy Cheesy Pretzel Bites

This recipe is a bit wild but turns out delicious. Kids are going to love it!

Servings: 12

Preparation Time: 2 Hours 30 Minutes

Ingredients:

- 1 (7g) package active dry yeast
- 1 c. warm water
- 1 tbsp. brown sugar
- 3 ¼ c. bread flour
- ½ c. cold milk
- 2 tbsp. unsalted butter, cut into 1" pieces plus extra for greasing
- 2 tsp. salt
- 1 ½ c. cheddar cheese, grated
- 1 c. chips of your choice, crushed
- 1 egg yolk + 1 tbsp. water - egg wash

Instructions:

Preheat your oven to 500°F.

In a stand mixer, add the warm water and active dry yeast.

Add in the brown sugar. Mix thoroughly and allow to bloom until foamy. It should take about 5 minutes.

Add in the bread flour, unsalted butter, cold milk and salt, then continue stirring. At low speed, begin kneading the dough for 1 minute or until it forms a smooth ball. Continue kneading until the dough become pliant about 5 minutes.

In a greased bowl, place the dough and cover it with saran wrap. Set away to rise in a warm area for 90 minutes until double in size. Divide the dough into 12 pieces.

Roll each piece into a rectangle. Place about 2 tablespoons of the cheddar cheese in the center and top with about 1 tablespoon of the chips.

Pull the edges together and pinch them to cover. Ensure the filling is completely covered and set onto a baking tray.

Repeat the process with the remaining dough rectangles. Place them 2" apart.

Allow rising for 30 more minutes.

Coat with the quick egg wash before baking for 10 minutes until crispy and golden brown!

16. Sparkling White Chocolate Pretzels

Add some sparkle and glitz to your seasonal spread this year with these glittering white chocolate pretzels.

Servings: 5

Preparation Time: 15 Minutes

Ingredients:

- 8 oz. white chocolate baking bars, chopped
- 10 oz. packaged pretzel rods
- Colored sparkling sugar and edible glitter sprinkles as needed

Instructions:

In a bowl, melt the white chocolate baking bars for 60 seconds in your microwave. Stir.

Microwave for another 20 seconds stirring until combined and smooth.

Dip each pretzel rod approximately halfway into the chocolate, allowing any excess to drip off.

Sprinkle colored sparkling sugar and edible glitter sprinkles over the top and transfer to waxed paper to set.

17. Strawberry Layered Pretzel Dessert

Your younger guests will especially love this dessert. Thanks to its pretzel base, it's colorful and fruity and has excellent texture.

Servings: 5

Preparation Time: 6 Hours 30 Minutes

Ingredients:

- 8 oz. pretzels, crushed
- ¾ c. butter, melted
- 3 tbsp. granulated sugar

Filling:

- 2 c. whipped topping
- 8 oz. cream cheese, softened
- 1 c. sugar

Topping:

- 2 c. boiling water
- 2 - 3 oz. packaged strawberry gelatin
- 2 - 16 oz. packaged frozen sweetened strawberries, sliced (thawed)
- Whipped topping
- Pretzels

Instructions:

Combine the pretzels with the butter and granulated sugar in a bowl.

Press the mixture gently but firmly into an ungreased 13 by 9" baking dish. Then, bake in the oven at 350°F for 10 minutes. Cool on a wire baking rack.

Begin preparing the filling: In a bowl, beat the whipped topping with the cream cheese and sugar until silky smooth. Spread the mixture evenly over the pretzel base and transfer to the fridge until chilled.

For the topping, add the boiling water to a bowl. Scatter over the strawberry gelatin to dissolve.

Stir in the frozen sweetened strawberries, then chill until partially set.

Spoon the mixture over the filling and chill for 6 hours until firm.

Cut into squares, then serve with whipped topping and pretzels.

18. Strawberry Pretzel Party Popsicles

These party popsicles will keep kids happy, leaving grown-ups free to socialize.

Servings: 5

Preparation Time: 1 Hour

Ingredients:

- 8 strawberries, hulled and chopped
- 1 tbsp. strawberry jam
- ½ c. plain Greek yogurt
- 1 tbsp. runny honey
- 1 tsp. vanilla extract
- 4 hard-shell pretzels, chopped very small

Instructions:

Add the strawberries to a bowl.

Add the strawberry jam to the strawberries, then toss to coat evenly. Put aside.

Combine the plain Greek yogurt with the runny honey and vanilla extract in a bowl.

Add 1 tablespoon to the yogurt mixture in a popsicle mold.

Layer the mold with the strawberries and hard-shell pretzels. Repeat until the mold is full. The final layer should be the yogurt mixture.

Transfer to the freezer until solid.

19. Swedish Sugared Sweet Pretzels

The butter and sugar coating is all it takes to make these Swedish pretzels sweet perfection.

Servings: 5

Preparation Time: 1 Hour 30 Minutes

Ingredients:

- ½ c. warm milk at 115°F
- 1 tbsp. active dry yeast
- 1 ½ c. + 1 tsp. sugar, divided
- 2 eggs
- 3 ¾ c. flour
- ¼ tsp. salt
- 1 tbsp. baking powder
- ¾ tsp. ground cardamom
- ½ c. + 2 tbsp. unsalted butter at room temperature, cubed
- 6 tbsp. butter, melted

Instructions:

In a bowl that has paddle attachment, mix the warm milk with the active dry yeast and 1 teaspoon of the sugar. Allow standing for 5 minutes until foamy.

Add the baking powder, ground cardamom, eggs, flour, salt and ¼ cup of the sugar. Mix at moderate speed. You will need to scrape the bowl's sides for approximately 2 minutes or until the dough forms.

Add ½ cup of the unsalted butter. Then, mix for around 5 minutes until a dough comes together and is shiny and smooth.

Mold the dough into a ball, then cover it with kitchen wrap.

Set the dough aside for 60 minutes, at room temperature, until doubled in size.

On a floured clean work surface and with a lightly floured rolling pin, roll the dough out into an 8 by 12" rectangle shape, with the 12" side on your front.

Evenly spread the rest of the unsalted butter over the bottom half of the dough.

Carefully fold the buttered half of the dough over the top half, pressing down gently to create a rectangle of approximately 4 by 12". Then, cut the dough crosswise into 12 1" wide strips.

Roll each strip into a 12" long rope.

Next, create the pretzels. Shape each rope into a u-shape, then cross the ends over each other, twisting and pressing them down to create a pretzel shape.

Arrange the pretzels approximately 1" apart on 2 baking sheets lined with parchment paper.

Cover the pretzels with a tea towel and set them aside to rest for approximately 30 minutes.

Preheat the main oven to 425°F.

Bake the pretzels for 15 minutes, turning the sheets once until a pale golden color.

Allow cooling slightly.

Add the remaining sugar to a bowl.

Add the butter to a second bowl.

While the pretzels are warm, brush them all over with the butter and roll them in the sugar to evenly and well coat.

Transfer to a cooling rack.

Serve and enjoy.

20. White Chocolate and Pink Peppercorn Pretzels

Pink peppercorns add a festive fruity spice twist to this sweet snack.

Servings: 5

Preparation Time: 1 Hour 15 Minutes

Ingredients:

- 11 oz. white chocolate chips
- 9 oz. mini pretzels
- 2 tbsp. pink peppercorns, crushed

Instructions:

Melt the white chocolate chips over moderate heat while whisking continually until smooth for approximately 2 minutes using a double boiler.

Add the mini pretzels to the chocolate. Then, toss until evenly coated.

Evenly divide the pretzels on 2 waxed paper lined cookie sheets.

Sprinkle the pink peppercorns over the pretzels. Then, place in the fridge to chill and set for approximately 30-40 minutes.

21. White Chocolate Haystacks

These white chocolate pretzel haystacks are a delicious treat that is wonderfully simple to make – what's not to love?!

Servings: 5

Preparation Time: 30 Minutes

Ingredients:

- ½ c. pretzel sticks
- ½ c. puffed crispy rice cereal
- ½ c. salty peanuts
- 4 oz. white baking chocolate, roughly chopped
- 1 tsp. shortening

Instructions:

Combine the pretzel sticks, puffed crispy rice cereal and salty peanuts in a large bowl.

Cover your cookie sheet with wax paper.

Melt together the white chocolate and shortening using your microwave. Stir until silky.

Pour the chocolate over the pretzel mixture. Then, fold gently until evenly coated.

Drop tablespoonfuls onto the wax paper in heaps. Put to one side until set.

22. Yogurt Glazed Pretzels

These yogurt-glazed mini pretzels make the perfect party snack for kids. They are healthy and delicious, and better yet, you can use different flavor yogurts.

Servings: 5

Preparation Time: 5 Hours

Ingredients:

- 5 c. powdered sugar
- 2 c. vanilla yogurt
- 40 mini hard-shell pretzels

Instructions:

Preheat the main oven to 250°F.

Use a hand blender to mix the powdered sugar with the vanilla yogurt in a bowl.

Using kitchen tongs, dip the mini hard-shell pretzels, one by one, into the sugar frosting until generously coated and arrange them on a wire baking rack. Set the rack on a cookie sheet to make cleaning up easier.

Once the pretzels are all coated, turn the oven off. Then, place the sheet in the oven, with the oven door partially open for 4 hours. It will allow the frosting to set and prevent the pretzels from becoming soggy.

Remove the pretzels from the oven, then store them in a resealable airtight container for up to 72 hours.

23. Vegan Heart

When you are a vegan, it does not mean that you need to forget about your sweet tooth! We all have our dessert cravings, no matter what diet one follows. And, not giving in to the cravings just doesn't sound right, does it? But that is why this recipe is a godsend! The pretzels are soft and doughy and give a naturally sweet taste, perfect for your sweet cravings, and they are shaped into a heart!

Servings: 12

Preparation Time: 30 Minutes

Ingredients:

- 2 tbsp. maple syrup
- 1 c. unsweetened non-dairy milk
- 1 (7g) pack active dry yeast
- 2 bananas
- 1 c. refined flour
- 1 c. whole wheat flour
- ¼ c. natural peanut butter
- 1 1/8 tsp. ground cinnamon
- ¼ tsp. ground nutmeg
- ½ tsp. salt
- 5 c. water
- 1 tsp. vegetable oil
- 5 tbsp. baking soda
- 2 tsp. coarse sea salt

Instructions:

Preheat your oven to 450°F.

In a saucepan, heat the unsweetened non-dairy milk until warm. Add in the maple syrup along with the active dry yeast. Let the mixture rest for 10 minutes or until it starts to foam.

Take ¾ of the yeast mixture and crush the bananas into it. Add the natural peanut butter to it, then mix well. Stir in the salt, ground cinnamon, ground nutmeg and flours along with the remaining yeast mixture. Combine until a dough starts to form.

Sprinkle some flour on the surface. Place the dough on it and knead it for 10-15 minutes.

Place the dough in a bowl smeared with oil and cover it with plastic wrap. Let the dough rest for 60 minutes or until it increases in its size.

Now, make 8 equal divisions of the dough and roll each division into a 18" long rope. Then, carefully twist the ends over each other and shape them into a heart.

In a pan, boil the water mixed in with the baking soda. Meanwhile, take a baking sheet and line it with parchment paper.

Mix the vegetable oil, coarse sea salt and maple syrup in a bowl.

Dip each pretzel into the boiling water for 30 seconds. Place the pretzels on the baking sheet and slice the top of the pretzels twice or thrice. Brush them with the maple syrup mixture.

Place the pretzels into the oven. Bake them for 15 minutes or until they turn golden brown.

Serve warm!

24. The Herbal Knot

Pretzels are delicious as they are. However, they taste ravishing with a few alterations made to the standard recipe. These pretzels are the perfect example of it. They are made following the same classic pretzel recipe, with the much-needed addition of herbs to give you the satisfaction of having the taste of salt and herbs all in one bite!

Servings: 12

Preparation Time: 1 Hour 30 Minutes

Ingredients:

- 3 c. refined flour
- 1 c. white whole wheat flour
- 1 ¼ tsp. salt
- 1 tbsp. yeast
- ½ c. water
- 1 c. milk
- 1 tbsp. honey
- ¼ tsp. dried parsley
- ¼ tsp. dried oregano
- ¼ tsp. dried basil
- ½ tsp. garlic powder
- ¼ c. baking soda
- 2 c. water
- 2 tbsp. sesame seeds
- 2 tsp. coarse sea salt

Instructions:

Preheat your oven to 450°F.

In a pan, warm ½ cup of the water, the milk, yeast and honey. Let the mixture sit for 5 minutes, then add the salt, dried herbs, garlic powder and flours. Knead until a dough has formed well.

Place the dough in a bowl smeared with oil. Cover it with plastic wrap and let it rest for 60 minutes.

Now, make 8 equal divisions of the dough and roll each division into a 18" long rope. Then, carefully twist the ends over each other and shape them into a pretzel knot.

In a pan, boil 2 cups of the water mixed in with the baking soda. Meanwhile, take a baking sheet and line it with parchment paper.

Dip each pretzel knot into the boiling water for 30 seconds. Place the pretzels on the baking sheet and slice the top of the pretzels twice or thrice. Sprinkle the coarse sea salt and sesame seeds over them.

Place the pretzels into the oven. Bake them for 15 minutes or until they turn golden brown.

Serve warm!

25. The Perfect Appetizer

If you are in a group of people who need to have an excellent appetizer to present before the guests, then this recipe is the one for you! So, the next time you have your guest coming over, remember to whip out it to make the most delicious appetizer ever!

Servings: 20

Preparation Time: 50 Minutes

Ingredients:

- 1 c. chicken, shredded
- 1 (3 lb.) pack soft buttery pretzel mix
- 4 oz. havarti cheese
- 2 tsp. ranch dressing
- 3 tbsp. buffalo wing sauce
- 2 c. water
- ¼ c. baking soda

Instructions:

Preheat your oven to 400°F.

Make the pretzel dough according to the instructions given on the pack. Then, place it in an oil-smeared bowl and cover it with plastic wrap.

Meanwhile, add the chicken with the buffalo wing sauce. Mix well.

Sprinkle some flour on a surface and place the dough on it. Divide the dough into small balls that fit into your palm perfectly. Flatten the balls, then add the havarti cheese and chicken mixture to each ball. Carefully pinch them close.

In a pan, boil the water mixed in with the baking soda. Meanwhile, take a baking sheet and line it with parchment paper.

Dip each roll into the boiling water for 30 seconds. Then, place the rolls on the baking sheet.

Place the rolls into the oven. Bake them for 15 minutes or until they turn golden brown.

Serve warm with the ranch dressing!

26. The Big Delight

Regular pretzels are amazing. We all love them! Now, imagine having the same soft and doughy pretzels in a few sizes more significant!

Servings: 6

Preparation Time: 30 Minutes

Ingredients:

- 2 ¼ cups refined flour
- 1 tsp. kosher salt
- 3 tbsp. brown sugar
- 2 ½ c. water
- 1 c. milk
- 1 (7g) pack active dry yeast
- 1/3 c. baking soda
- 10 tbsp. unsalted butter
- 2 tsp. coarse sea salt
- ½ c. butter, melted

Sauce:

- 2 tsp. mustard
- 2 tbsp. brown sugar
- 2 tbsp. vinegar
- 1 c. mayonnaise

Instructions:

Preheat your oven to 450°F.

Take a saucepan and warm the milk in it. In a bowl, add in the milk along with the active dry yeast. Let the mixture rest for 4-5 minutes. Now, pour in the refined flour, kosher salt, unsalted butter and brown sugar. Mix well.

Place the dough in a bowl smeared with oil. Cover it with plastic wrap and let it rest for 60 minutes.

Sprinkle some flour on a counter. Then, place the dough and divide it into 6 equal pieces. Roll each piece into a 30" long rope. Shape the ropes into a pretzel knot.

In a pan, boil the water mixed in with the baking soda. Meanwhile, take a baking sheet and line it with parchment paper.

Dip each roll into the boiling water for 30 seconds. Then, place the rolls on the baking sheet and sprinkle them with the coarse sea salt.

Put the rolls into the oven. Then, bake them for 15 minutes or until they turn golden brown.

Now, dip the pretzels into a bowl of the butter. Remove them and let the excess butter fall off.

Mix the mustard, brown sugar, vinegar and mayonnaise in a bowl for the sauce. Place the bowl in the refrigerator.

Serve warm with the sauce!

27. Mini Coco Bites

Eating chocolates as a snack is something that we all do. So, what better to put chocolate in pretzels? The salty and sweet taste provided by pretzels will be heightened to the max with a delicious combo of Hershey's and M&M! So, bring out those packets of chocolate that you have and get ready to make this delicious combo!

Servings: 50

Preparation Time: 20 Minutes

Ingredients:

- 50 M&M milk chocolate
- 50 square pretzel bites
- 50 Hershey's hugs

Instructions:

Preheat your oven to 200°F.

Line a baking sheet with parchment paper. Place the square pretzel bites on the sheet and put one Hershey's hug on each bite.

Bake for 5 minutes.

Take the sheet out. Then, place one M&M milk chocolate on each Hershey's hug topped pretzel. Press down carefully.

Put the pretzels into the freezer for approximately 10 minutes.

Serve them or store them for later!

28. The Classic Cheese Pretzels

Cheese!!!! Just the name of it is enough to have your mouth watering, isn't it? Especially if you stuff it into something soft and doughy. Now, pizza is a go-to when you think about cheese and dough, but we don't always have the time to bake a pizza. Therefore, it makes this recipe is perfect for people who love cheese all stuffed into a dough, one which you can bite and get that delicious stretch of cheese oozing out! Especially from the sweet and savory pretzels!

Servings: 8

Preparation Time: 1 Hour 30 Minutes

Ingredients:

- 4 ¼ c. refined flour, plus more for dusting
- 2 tsp. kosher salt
- 1 tbsp. sugar
- 2 ½ c. warm water
- 1 c. cheddar cheese, shredded
- 2 ½ tsp. active dry yeast
- 2/3 c. baking soda
- 3 ½ tbsp. unsalted butter
- 2 quarts water
- 1 egg yolk + 1 tbsp. water - egg wash
- 2 tsp. coarse sea salt

Instructions:

Preheat your oven to 400°F.

In a stand mixer, combine the active dry yeast in the warm water. Let the mixture rest for 1 minute, then add the refined flour, kosher salt, unsalted butter and sugar into it. Combine at low speed. Increase the speed once the dough has combined enough to medium. Mix the dough for 5 minutes or until it pulls away from the bowl's surface.

Place the dough in a bowl smeared with oil. Cover it with wrap and let it rest for 60 minutes.

Sprinkle little refined flour on the counter and place the dough on it. Make 8 equal divisions of the dough. Roll them into a 18" long log. Flatten the logs, then spread the cheddar cheese along their lengths. Carefully shape them into a pretzel knot.

In a pan, boil the water mixed in with the baking soda. Meanwhile, take a baking sheet and line it with parchment paper.

Dip each roll into the boiling water for 30 seconds. Transfer the rolls to your baking sheet and brush them with the egg wash. Sprinkle the coarse sea salt.

Bake until the pretzels turn golden brown for 15 minutes.

Serve warm!

29. Pretzel Pie

Taking desserts is an essential complement to any meal. You do not need to have a sweet tooth to take this pie. But who can resist a plate of pie?

Servings: 8

Preparation Time: 30 Minutes

Ingredients:

- ½ c. butter, melted
- 1 ¼ c. pretzels, crushed
- ¼ c. granulated sugar
- 1 (2 lb.) pack strawberry flavored gelatin
- 1 ½ c. heavy cream
- ¾ c. boiling water
- ¾ c. powdered sugar
- 1 tsp. lime peel, grated
- ¼ c. lime juice
- 2 c. strawberries, slightly crushed

Instructions:

Add the pretzels, butter and granulated sugar to a bowl. Mix well. Then, flatten the mixture at the bottom of a pie plate.

In a different bowl, dissolve the strawberry flavored gelatin in the boiling water. Add the lime peel and lime juice. Then, refrigerate the mixture for 1 hour.

Beat the gelatin mixture until it becomes thick and fluffy using an electric mixer. In a bowl, beat the heavy cream and powdered sugar until foam begins to form.

Mix the strawberries and whipped cream into the gelatin mixture. Then, transfer the mixture to the pie plate.

Refrigerate for at least 8 hours.

30. Pretzel Cake

This cake is a treat that anyone can take at any time and place. However, you may not be sure when the cravings kick in, making the recipe is a top pick. It is simple to make and requires few ingredients.

Servings: 12

Preparation Time: 20 Minutes

Ingredients:

- ¾ c. pretzels, crushed
- 2 tbsp. light treacle
- ½ c. milk chocolate
- 2 tbsp. butter

Instructions:

Boil water in a saucepan.

On the saucepan, place a heatproof bowl. Add in the milk chocolate, light treacle and butter. Stir to aid in melting the ingredients.

Remove the bowl from the saucepan, then add the pretzels. Stir to mix.

In a muffin tin, place muffin cases.

Pour the pretzel mixture into every case.

Refrigerate for about 1 hour.

Serve!

31. Pretzel Eggs

This recipe is excellent for children. You can spice the dish up by adding meat, cheese and vegetables.

Servings: 4

Preparation Time: 10 Minutes

Ingredients:

- 8 egg, beaten
- 1 tbsp. butter
- 1 ½ c. mini pretzels

Instructions:

In a skillet, add the butter, then melt it over medium heat.

Add the mini pretzels and eggs into the skillet, then cook as you stir the mixture occasionally.

Serve when hot.

32. Pretzel Bratwurst Bites

Place bratwurst slices at the center of pretzel bites and come up with a delicious and unique snack. This recipe is simple to make as you need to prepare it using pizza dough. Then, serve the bites with mustard.

Servings: 36

Preparation Time: 35 Minutes

Ingredients:

- 6 c. water
- ⅓ c. baking soda
- 8 oz. packaged refrigerated pizza dough
- 12 smoked bratwurst links
- ¼ tsp. kosher salt
- Mustard for serving

Instructions:

Preheat your oven to 450°F.

Grease your baking sheet lightly.

In a saucepan, dissolve the baking soda in the water, then allow the mixture to boil.

Roll the refrigerated pizza dough to form a 10 by 12" rectangle.

Cut the dough rectangle into 1" 12 strips, then use the strips to wrap the smoked bratwursts in a spiral form.

To seal, pinch the edges, then leave both ends about ½" open.

Dip the wrapped bratwursts into boiling water for half a minute, then transfer them to the baking sheet.

Sprinkle the wrapped bratwursts with the kosher salt.

Bake for 12 minutes in the oven until the bratwursts turn golden brown.

Divide the bratwursts into thirds.

Serve alongside mustard.

33. Homemade Pretzels

This recipe is fun to prepare and turns out delicious. Try it on those weekend mornings and afternoons.

Servings: 12

Preparation Time: 1 Hour 40 Minutes

Ingredients:

- 25 oz. packaged active dry yeast
- 1 c. warm water at 110°F
- 3 ½ c. all-purpose flour, plus more for dusting
- 2 tbsp. white sugar
- 1 tbsp. shortening, melted
- 1 tsp. salt
- 1 egg yolk
- 1 tbsp. water
- Coarse salt for topping

Instructions:

In a bowl, add the active dry yeast, then dissolve it with the warm water.

Add the shortening, white sugar, all-purpose flour and salt into the yeast mixture. Beat the mixture to make a dough.

Knead your dough on a flat surface with some all-purpose flour for about 5 minutes.

Transfer the dough into a greased bowl, then allow it to rise. Make sure it is in a warm place.

After 1 hour, punch the dough down, then divide it into 12 pieces.

Roll each piece to form a rope of about 19" long.

Preheat your oven to 375°F.

Grease a baking sheet.

Shape the ropes into a pretzel, then put them on the baking sheet.

Allow the pretzels to rest for about 4 minutes.

In a bowl, beat the water together with the egg yolk.

Brush the mixture over the pretzels, then sprinkle them with coarse salt.

Bake the pretzels for 15 minutes until they turn golden brown.

Serve and enjoy.

34. Pretzel Salad

This recipe is simple and has a decorative three-layer salad with pretzel crust, strawberry Jell-O topping and cream cheese center. The result is delicious.

Servings: 18

Preparation Time: 4 Hours 53 Minutes

Ingredients:

- 2 c. pretzels, crushed
- ¾ c. margarine, melted
- 2 tsp. white sugar
- 8 oz. packaged cream cheese
- ¾ c. white sugar
- 4 ½ oz. frozen whipped topping (thawed)
- 6 oz. packaged strawberry flavored Jell-O®
- 2 c. boiling water
- 10 oz. packaged frozen strawberries

Instructions:

Preheat your oven to 400°F.

In a bowl, mix the pretzels, margarine and 2 teaspoons of the white sugar.

Press the mixture into a 9 by 13" baking dish's bottom.

Bake for 8 minutes in the oven. Then, remove the mixture and let it cool.

Blend ¾ cup of the white sugar and the cream cheese, then add the frozen whipped topping. Mix well. Spread the mixture over the pretzel mixture evenly.

Add the strawberry flavored gelatin to the boiling water in a bowl, then let it dissolve.

Add the frozen strawberries. Then, set the mixture aside and let it cool for 15 minutes.

Pour the gelatin mixture over the cream mixture. Then, place in the refrigerator for 4 hours.

Serve and enjoy.

35. Pretzel Bread

This bread has tender texture resembling a pretzel. It also has a salty brown crust making it best for sandwiches.

Servings: 12

Preparation Time: 1 Hour 49 Minutes

Ingredients:

Dough:

- 2 tbsp. butter
- 1 c. milk
- 2 tbsp. brown sugar
- 1 (¼ oz.) envelope Fleischmann's® RapidRise yeast
- 2 tsp. salt
- 3 c. all-purpose flour
- 1 egg + 1 tsp. water - egg wash

Boiling Solution:

- ¾ c. baking soda
- 3 quarts water

Instructions:

Heat the butter and milk at 100°F until it becomes warm, but the butter does not melt completely.

In a bowl, mix the undissolved yeast and brown sugar, then add 2 cups of the all-purpose flour and the salt. Beat everything for 3 minutes.

Add enough all-purpose flour to prepare a soft dough. Knead the dough on a floured flat surface until it is elastic and smooth for 10 minutes.

Transfer the dough to a greased bowl. Cover it and let it rise for 1 hour.

Preheat your oven to 400°F.

Bring the boiling solution to a boil in a pot.

Punch your dough down, then divide it into 2 equal pieces. Form a smooth ball from each piece. Place the balls in the solution to boil for about 2 minutes as you turn them halfway. Using a slotted spoon, remove the balls, then place them on a greased baking sheet.

Brush the loaves with the egg wash, then cut across the top.

Bake for 15 minutes, then set the oven's temperature to 350°F. Bake for extra 12 minutes until the loaves begin to turn brown evenly.

Remove from the oven, then place on a wire rack to cool.

Serve and enjoy.

36. Sugar Pretzels

This recipe is a variation of the traditional cookie and has excellent taste. The pretzels are fun to prepare and make a great ornament for the Christmas tree, and you can present them as a gift.

Servings: 12

Preparation Time: 1 Hour 45 Minutes

Ingredients:

- 7 tbsp. unsalted butter
- 3 tbsp. white sugar
- 1 egg yolk
- 1 egg
- 1 ⅞ c. unbleached all-purpose flour
- 1 pinch salt
- ¼ tsp. ground black pepper
- 2 lemons
- ½ tsp. water
- ½ c. crystal sugar
- 1 egg yolk

Instructions:

In a bowl, beat the white sugar and unsalted butter together. Grate the lemon rinds finely, then add them to the mixture. Beat in the egg and egg yolk. Sift together the salt, ground black pepper and unbleached all-purpose flour, then add the mixture to the butter mixture. A dough is formed, and it is stiff.

Knead your dough on a flat surface until it forms an 8" long log shape with flat ends. Wrap it in airtight plastic wrap, then allow it to stand for 1 hour at room temperature.

Preheat your oven to 350°F.

Using aluminum foil, line cookie sheets.

Divide the dough equally into 12 pieces, then cover the pieces with plastic wrap.

Roll one piece on a floured surface for a 10 by 11" long roll tapered slightly at the ends.

Cross both ends about 2" from the ends as you bring them to the opposite side to form a pretzel shape. Dab under the ends with some water, then place them on the cookie sheets at 2" intervals.

In a bowl, mix the water and egg yolk.

Brush the yolk mixture over the pretzels, then sprinkle them with the crystal sugar.

Bake for 30 minutes as you ensure that you reverse the cookie sheets front to back and top to bottom once during the process.

When the pretzels turn golden brown, remove them, then place them on a cooling rack.

Serve and enjoy.

37. Pretzel Buns

These buns resemble and taste like a soft pretzel. They are simple to prepare and are perfect for sandwiches. You can try the buns with honey mustard and Swiss cheese.

Servings: 12

Preparation Time: 1 Hour 53 Minutes

Ingredients:

- 4 ½ tsp. active dry yeast
- 1 tsp. white sugar
- ½ c. warm water
- 2 c. warm milk
- 6 tbsp. vegetable shortening
- 2 eggs
- 6 c. all-purpose flour, divided
- 1 tbsp. vegetable oil, plus more for greasing
- ¼ c. white sugar
- 1 ½ tsp. salt
- ½ c. baking soda
- 4 c. hot water
- ¼ c. butter, melted
- Sea salt for topping

Instructions:

Add the warm water to a bowl, then dissolve the active dry yeast and 1 teaspoon of the white sugar in it. Let the water be below 100°F. Let the mixture stand for 5 minutes until it forms a creamy foam, and the yeast becomes soft.

Add the vegetable oil, vegetable shortening, eggs, warm milk, 1 ½ teaspoons of the salt, ¼ cup of the white sugar and 3 cups of all-purpose flour. Use an electric mixer to blend until everything becomes smooth on medium speed.

Use your hands to mix in the remaining all-purpose flour in bits until the dough gets to pull together.

Knead your dough on a flat surface until it is elastic and smooth for 5 minutes. Dip the dough in a lightly oiled bowl, then turn it to ensure it coats with the oil.

Cover the dough with a light cloth, then leave it to rise for 1 hour in a warm place of about 95°F.

Uncover the dough, then punch it down.

Preheat your oven to 350°F.

Pull off dough balls from the dough, then roll some of them to form a rope about 6" long.

Roll the ropes into a spiral to texture the top. Place the ready buns aside.

In a bowl, mix 4 cups of the hot water and the baking soda. Dip the buns in the mixture before transferring them onto a baking sheet.

Brush the buns with the butter, then sprinkle them with sea salt.

Bake for 25 minutes until the buns turn brown.

Remove the buns, then place them on a cooling rack.

Serve and enjoy.

38. Gluten-Free Pretzels

These pretzels are crunchy and tasty. You can include them in buffets during parties or get-togethers.

Servings: 12

Preparation Time: 2 Hours 2 Minutes

Ingredients:

- 2 ¼ tsp. active dry yeast
- 1 c. warm water
- 3 tbsp. light corn syrup
- 1 egg
- 2 tbsp. vegetable oil
- 2 c. white rice flour, plus more for dusting
- 1 c. brown rice flour
- ½ c. potato starch
- ¼ c. tapioca flour
- 1 tsp. salt
- 1 tsp. xanthan gum
- ½ tsp. baking powder
- 4 quarts water (optional)
- ¼ c. baking soda
- 2 tbsp. white sugar
- 2 tbsp. butter, melted
- Salt for topping

Instructions:

In a bowl, add the active dry yeast, then dissolve it in the warm water. Let the mixture stand for 5 minutes to form a creamy foam, and the yeast becomes soft. Add the vegetable oil, egg and light corn syrup, then whisk.

Whisk the brown rice flour, potato starch, white rice flour, salt, xanthan gum, baking powder and tapioca flour in a bowl. Whisk with an electric mixer that has a dough hook.

Add the yeast mixture into the bowl, then mix for 4 minutes at moderate speed until everything combines well.

Turn the dough on a work surface with light flour dusting, then knead it for 5 minutes until smooth. Place it into a lightly greased bowl, then cover it with plastic wrap. Let the dough rise for 1 hour.

Push the dough down to deflate it, then divide it into 12 equal portions. Roll each portion to form a 15" long rope, then shape it into a 'U.' To form a pretzel shape, twist both ends of the rope, then press the ends firmly into the top of the loop.

Preheat your oven to 425°F.

Grease 2 baking sheets.

Add the water into a pot, then bring it to a boil. Add the white sugar and baking soda carefully as the water foams vigorously. Dip the pretzels into the mixture, then remove them using a slotted spoon when they float on the water. Place the pretzels on the baking sheets.

Brush the pretzels with the butter, then finish by sprinkling salt on them.

Bake for 50 minutes until the pretzels begin to turn golden brown. Ensure you rotate the baking sheets halfway through the baking.

When ready, transfer the pretzels to a cooling rack.

Serve and enjoy.

39. DSF's Pretzel Bread

This recipe is perfect for pretzel lovers. You can prepare it to result in various forms. Nonetheless, the products have fantastic taste.

Servings: 6

Preparation Time: 1 Hour 10 Minutes

Ingredients:

- 1 tbsp. dark brown sugar
- 1 tbsp. honey (optional)
- 25 oz. packaged active dry yeast
- 1 c. warm water at 100 to 110°F
- 3 tbsp. unsalted butter, melted
- 2 tbsp. half-and-half
- 1 ½ tsp. salt
- 2 c. bread flour
- 1 tsp. unsalted butter, melted
- Cooking spray
- 1 c. water
- 5 tbsp. baking soda
- 3 tbsp. honey
- ½ tsp. salt

Instructions:

In a bowl with the warm water, dissolve the active dry yeast, dark brown sugar and 1 tablespoon of the honey. Let the mixture stand for 10 minutes until a foamy layer forms. Add the half and half, 1 ½ teaspoons of the salt and 3 tablespoons of the unsalted butter. Stir.

Add 1 cup of the bread flour to the mixture, then beat it to form a wet and sloppy dough.

On a floured surface, knead the dough as you add the remaining bread flour gradually until the dough becomes slightly sticky.

Grease a bowl with 1 teaspoon of the unsalted butter, then place the dough in it. Turn the dough to coat it with the butter. Cover it using plastic wrap, then let it rise for 1 hour.

Preheat your oven to 450°F.

Using cooking spray, grease a baking sheet.

In a pot of the water, add 3 tablespoons of the honey and the baking soda. Bring the mixture to a boil. Punch your dough down, then divide it into 2 pieces. Make loaves out of the pieces. Dip the loaves carefully into the boiling mixture, then cook for half a minute.

When the loaves float, remove them, then let them drain the excess water.

Place the loaves on the baking sheet. Then, sprinkle them with ½ teaspoons of the salt.

Using a knife, make an X cut on the loaves.

Bake on center rack for 10 minutes, then set the temperature to 400°F and continue baking for extra 10 minutes until the crust becomes brown and shiny.

Serve and enjoy.

40. Betty's Pretzels

These pretzels are a good gift for parties and other events. They only take 2 hours to be ready in a fantastic outcome.

Servings: 12

Preparation Time: 2 Hours

Ingredients:

- 24 oz. bite-size pretzels
- 1 oz. packaged dry onion soup mix
- 1 c. butter, melted

Instructions:

Preheat your oven to 275°F.

In a bowl, mix the butter and dry onion soup mix. Add the bite-size pretzels, then toss the mixture to allow it to coat. Spread the coated pretzels in a baking dish's bottom.

Bake for 1 hour as you stir after every 15 minutes. Allow the pretzels to cool completely before storing them in an airtight container.

41. Bacon-Wrapped Pretzels

Any recipe with bacon never goes wrong, as this dish will leave you yearning for more. You can serve the pretzels with a dipping of warm chocolate sauce.

Servings: 20

Preparation Time: 30 Minutes

Ingredients:

- 1 c. brown sugar
- 3 tbsp. red chili powder
- 1 pinch cayenne pepper
- 12 oz. packaged bacon, thinly sliced
- 15 oz. packaged short pretzel rods

Instructions:

Preheat your oven to 375°F.

Line a baking sheet using aluminum foil, then top it with a wire rack.

Mix the cayenne pepper, brown sugar and red chili powder in a bowl.

Dip the bacon slices in the mixture, then wrap them around the short pretzel rods leaving tiny spaces at the bottom to help handle the pretzel.

Arrange the pretzels on the wire rack.

Bake for 22 minutes until the bacon slices are crisp.

42. Chocolate Pretzels

These pretzels are unlike any you have ever had before! Try the recipe out to surprise your family with a delicious snack.

Servings: 24

Preparation Time: 12 Minutes

Ingredients:

- 69 oz. packaged mini candy-coated chocolates
- 24 milk chocolate candy kisses
- 24 circular pretzels

Instructions:

Preheat your oven to 350°F.

Arrange the circular pretzels on baking sheets, then unwrap the milk chocolate candy kisses. At the center of every pretzel, place the candy kisses.

Bake for around 3 minutes until the candy kisses melt.

Remove from the oven, then place one mini candy-coated chocolate in the center of every pretzel.

Refrigerate the pretzels until they are ready.

43. Pretzels with Coconut and Cream Cheese

This is a wonderful recipe if you want to diversify your diet and simply want to try something new.

Servings: 12

Preparation Time: 2 Hours 50 Minutes

Ingredients:

- 1 (7g) package active dry yeast
- 1 ½ c. cream cheese frosting
- 4 tbsp. coconut flakes
- 1 c. warm water
- ½ c. cold milk
- 2 tbsp. unsalted butter, plus extra for greasing
- 1 tbsp. brown sugar
- 3 ¼ c. bread flour
- 2 tsp. salt
- 2 tsp. sweetened coconut flakes for topping
- 1 egg + 1 tsp. water - egg wash

Instructions:

Prepare the oven by preheating it to 500°F.

Add the warm water to a stand mixer. Sprinkle the active dry yeast over the top.

Mix in the brown sugar. Then, let the mixture bloom for about 5 minutes and become foamy.

Stir in the salt, bread flour, cold milk and unsalted butter. Knead the dough at low speed to form a smooth ball for about 1 minute. Continue the kneading process for 5 minutes to form a pliant.

Lightly grease a bowl. Set in the dough ball and use saran wrap to cover it. Set it aside in a warm place for 90 minutes to allow it to rise and double.

Set the dough ball to a floured countertop and equally divide it into 12 portions.

Roll each portion to form a rectangle. Then, in the center, pipe 2 tbsp. of the cream cheese frosting and top with 1 tbsp. of the coconut flakes.

Wrap the edges and pinch them to seal. Then, put on a baking sheet.

Do the same for the remaining dough rectangles. You should allow some space of 2" apart between the pretzels.

Allow for extra 30 minutes to rise.

Brush with the egg wash to coat, then bake until golden brown and crispy for about 10 minutes.

You may add a topping of the sweetened coconut flakes. Serve and enjoy.

44. Caramel Pretzel Bites

For anyone who wants to try a healthier alternative to the traditional sweet and salty snack, this is the perfect recipe.

Servings: 12

Preparation Time: 2 Hours 30 Minutes

Ingredients:

- 1 (7g) package active dry yeast
- 3 ¼ c. bread flour
- 1 c. warm water
- ½ c. cold milk
- 2 tbsp. unsalted butter, plus extra for greasing
- 1 tbsp. brown sugar
- 2 tsp. salt
- 1 ½ c. store-bought caramel sauce
- 1 egg + 1 tsp. water - egg wash

Instructions:

Prepare the oven by preheating it to 500°F.

Add the warm water to a stand mixer. Sprinkle the active dry yeast over the top.

Mix in the brown sugar. Then, let the mixture bloom for about 5 minutes and become foamy.

Stir in the salt, bread flour, cold milk and unsalted butter. Knead the dough at low speed to form a smooth ball for about 1 minute. Continue the kneading process for 5 minutes to form a pliant.

Lightly grease a bowl. Set in the dough ball and use saran wrap to cover it. Set it aside in a warm place for 90 minutes to allow it to rise and double.

Set the dough ball to a floured countertop and equally divide it into 12 portions.

Roll each portion to form a rectangle. Then, in the center, add 2 tbsp. of the store-bought caramel sauce.

Wrap the edges and pinch them to seal. Then, put on a baking sheet.

Do the same for the remaining dough rectangles. You should allow some space of 2" apart between the pretzels.

Allow for extra 30 minutes to rise.

Brush with the egg wash to coat, then bake until golden brown and crispy for about 10 minutes.

45. Cheesy Garlic Pull Apart Pretzels

The combination of cheese and garlic is absolutely amazing! You will have your guests gobbling these pretzels up as soon as they're served!

Servings: 12

Preparation Time: 2 Hours 30 Minutes

Ingredients:

- 1 (7g) package active dry yeast
- 1 c. warm water
- 1 tbsp. brown sugar
- 3 ¼ c. bread flour
- ½ c. cold milk
- 2 tbsp. unsalted butter, plus extra for greasing
- 2 tsp. salt
- 24 mozzarella balls
- 1 tbsp. unsalted butter, melted
- 3 tbsp. garlic, chopped
- 3 tbsp. flat-leaf parsley, freshly chopped

Instructions:

Prepare the oven by preheating it to 500°F.

Add the warm water to a stand mixer. Sprinkle the active dry yeast over the top.

Mix in the brown sugar. Then, let the mixture bloom for about 5 minutes and become foamy.

Stir in the salt, bread flour, cold milk and 2 tbsp. of the unsalted butter. Knead the dough at low speed to form a smooth ball for about 1 minute. Continue the kneading process for 5 minutes to form a pliant.

Lightly grease a bowl. Set in the dough ball and use saran wrap to cover it. Set it aside in a warm place for 90 minutes to allow it to rise and double.

Set the dough ball to a floured countertop and equally divide it into 12 portions.

Make a 4" circle out of each portion.

The 2 mozzarella cheese balls should be cut in half and stacked in the middle of each circle.

Wrap the edges by pinching them together. Completely cover the cheese balls. Then, put on a lined baking pan after rolling in your hands to ensure a proper shape.

Do the same for the remaining dough circle. You should allow some space of 2" apart between the pretzels.

Allow for extra 30 minutes to rise, then bake for about 5 minutes

Remove from the oven. Apply a coating of 1 tbsp. of the unsalted butter and use the garlic to sprinkle over.

Take back in the oven and allow baking until golden brown and crispy for extra 5 minutes

Remove from the oven and apply a topping of the flat-leaf parsley. Serve and enjoy.

46. Parmesan Crusted Soft Pretzels

These pretzels have a traditional pretzel flavor but are much softer, making them easier to bite into.

Servings: 12

Preparation Time: 2 ½ Hours

Ingredients:

- 1 (7g) package active dry yeast
- 1 c. warm water
- 1 tbsp. brown sugar
- 3 ¼ c. bread flour
- ½ c. cold milk
- 2 tbsp. unsalted butter, plus extra for greasing
- 2 tsp. salt
- 1 c. parmesan cheese, grated
- 1 egg + 1 tsp. water - egg wash

Instructions:

Prepare the oven by preheating it to 500°F.

Add the warm water to a stand mixer. Sprinkle the active dry yeast over the top.

Mix in the brown sugar. Then, let the mixture bloom for about 5 minutes and become foamy.

Stir in the salt, bread flour, cold milk and unsalted butter. Knead the dough at low speed to form a smooth ball for about 1 minute. Continue the kneading process for 5 minutes to form a pliant.

Lightly grease a bowl. Set in the dough ball and use saran wrap to cover it. Set it aside in a warm place for 90 minutes to allow it to rise and double.

Divide into 8 portions and roll out into a desired shape – knots, buns or sticks.

Arrange on 2 lined baking trays about 2" apart.

Allow rising for 30 more minutes.

Brush with the egg wash to coat followed by a sprinkle of the parmesan cheese, then bake until golden brown and crispy for about 10 minutes.

Serve and enjoy!

47. Pizza Pretzel Bites

These pretzel bites practically have all the tastes of pizza, making them easy to feel full but still have your sweet tooth satisfied.

Servings: 12

Preparation Time: 2 ½ Hours

Ingredients:

- 1 (7g) package active dry yeast
- 1 c. warm water
- 1 tbsp. brown sugar
- 3 ¼ c. bread flour
- 2 tbsp. unsalted butter, plus extra for greasing
- 2 tsp. salt
- 1 c. pizza sauce
- 2 tbsp. olives, chopped
- ½ c. cheese, grated
- 1 egg + 1 tsp. water - egg wash

Instructions:

Prepare the oven by preheating it to 500°F.

Add the warm water to a stand mixer. Sprinkle the active dry yeast over the top.

Mix in the brown sugar. Then, let the mixture bloom for about 5 minutes and become foamy.

Stir in the salt, bread flour, cold milk and unsalted butter. Knead the dough at low speed to form a smooth ball for about 1 minute. Continue the kneading process for 5 minutes to form a pliant.

Lightly grease a bowl. Set in the dough ball and use saran wrap to cover it. Set it aside in a warm place for 90 minutes to allow it to rise and double.

Meanwhile, mix the olives and pizza sauce. Then, set aside.

Set the dough ball to a floured countertop and equally divide it into 12 portions.

Roll each portion to form a rectangle. Then, heat 2 tbsp. of the olive mixture in the center. Apply a topping of 1 tbsp. of the cheese.

Wrap the edges and pinch them to seal. Then, put on a baking sheet.

Do the same for the remaining dough rectangles. You should allow some space of 2" apart between the pretzels.

Allow for extra 30 minutes to rise.

Brush with the egg wash to coat, then bake until golden brown and crispy for about 10 minutes.

48. Pretzel Toffee

This is a dense and chewy sweet combination of toffee and pretzels, very much like the taste of the Heath bar.

Servings: 7

Preparation Time: 1 Hour

Ingredients:

- 2 c. pretzels
- 1 c. butter
- 1 c. light brown sugar
- 2 c. milk or dark chocolate chips

Instructions:

Prepare the oven by preheating it to 350°F. Line parchment paper to a cookie sheet.

Over the prepared cookie sheet, spread an even layer of the pretzels. Then, set aside.

Add the butter and light brown sugar to a pot and heat to melt. Cook the mixture on moderate heat for 8 minutes until browned.

Evenly pour the toffee mixture into the pretzels until well coated.

Set in the oven and bake for 10 minutes.

Remove from the oven. Then, apply a topping of the chocolate chips and let it melt for about 3 minutes. Use a spatula to spread well to ensure the topping evenly covers the toffee layer.

Let the toffee cool at room temperature to harden.

Break into a desired number of pieces. Set in an airtight container before storing in your refrigerator.

49. Peppermint Pretzel Dippers

Another delicious unique combination of pretzels, this treat is sure to make your guests beg for more.

Servings: 5

Preparation Time: 2 Hours

Ingredients:

- 2 c. semi-sweet chocolate chips
- 1 tbsp. shortening
- 40 red and green mint candies, crushed
- 10 oz. pretzel rods

Instructions:

Set the shortening and semi-sweet chocolate chips in a microwave and melt them. Stir well until they become silky.

Use wax paper to line a baking sheet. Then, set aside.

Using a plate, spread the red and green mint candies.

Snap the pretzel rods in half. Dip the snapped ends halfway in the chocolate for coating, then roll in the candies. Set on the baking sheet.

Chill until the chocolate sets.

50. Pineapple Pretzel Fluff

This is a great combination of pineapple and pretzels, making it a perfect snack for kids or anyone who wants something different.

Servings: 5

Preparation Time: 1 Hour

Ingredients:

- 1 c. pretzels, coarsely crushed
- ½ c. butter, melted
- 1 c. sugar, divided
- 8 oz. cream cheese at room temperature
- 1 (20 oz.) can unsweetened pineapple, crushed and drained
- 12 oz. frozen whipped topping, thawed

Instructions:

Prepare the oven by preheating it to 400°F.

Using a bowl, mix ½ cup of the sugar, the butter and pretzels. Firmly and gently press the mixture to a baking pan. Then, set in the oven to bake for about 8 minutes.

Remove from the oven and set on a wire rack to cool.

Meanwhile, beat the cream cheese and remaining sugar in a bowl to obtain a creamy and smooth mixture.

Apply the creamy and smooth mixture to the pretzel layer

Fold in the frozen whipped topping and unsweetened pineapple. Set your bowl in the refrigerator while covered until ready to serve.

Apply the pineapple mixture to the cream layer.

51. Coco Pretzels

These pretzels actually taste like a malted milk ball and are fun for those who want to try something new.

Servings: 8

Preparation Time: 45 Minutes

Ingredients:

- 4 ½ c. refined flour
- 2 ¼ tsp. active dry yeast
- 2 oz. butter
- 1 ½ c. warm water
- 1 tbsp. sugar
- 2 tsp. kosher salt
- 1 c. baking soda
- 2 quarts water
- ½ c. chocolate chips
- 1 egg
- 2 tbsp. vegetable oil
- 1 (4 oz.) pack pretzel salt
- 1 egg yolk + 1 tbsp. water - egg wash

Instructions:

Prepare the oven by preheating it to 450°F.

In a bowl, combine the warm water, sugar, active dry yeast and kosher salt. Set aside for 5 minutes.

Mix in the butter and refined flour.

Mix in the chocolate chips until well combined with the dough.

Smear a bowl with the vegetable oil. Set in the dough. Then, allow to rest for 60 minutes while covered.

Set the dough on a floured countertop and divide it into 8 portions.

Roll each portion into an 18" long rope. Twist the ends over each other and shape them into a pretzel knot.

Mix the water and baking soda and boil in a pan.

Line parchment paper on a baking sheet.

Dip each pretzel into the boiling water for 30 seconds. Set the pretzels on the baking sheet. Then, brush with the egg wash and sprinkle with the pretzel salt.

Set in the oven to bake until golden brown for 15 minutes.

Serve while warm.

Conclusion

This cookbook is a great way to get ideas and is designed to be straightforward. It also gives you some brilliant alternatives if you just need inspiration. Overall, it is a great book that can benefit anyone who loves pretzels as much as you do. If you're looking for something new to try with your family or friends, the cookbook will be the ideal choice for you.

Epilogues

There are days I feel like quitting, but then I remember readers like you, and my heart swells with pride at the love you show me by buying each and every book I put out there.

I am delighted, to say the least, to know that people like you take their time to download, read and cook with my books!

Thank you so much for accepting me and all that I have shared with the world.

While I am basking in the euphoria of your love and commitment to my books, I would beseech you to kindly drop your reviews and feedback. I would love to read from you!

Head to Amazon.com to drop your reviews!!!

Thank you

Charlotte Long

Made in the USA
Monee, IL
13 November 2022